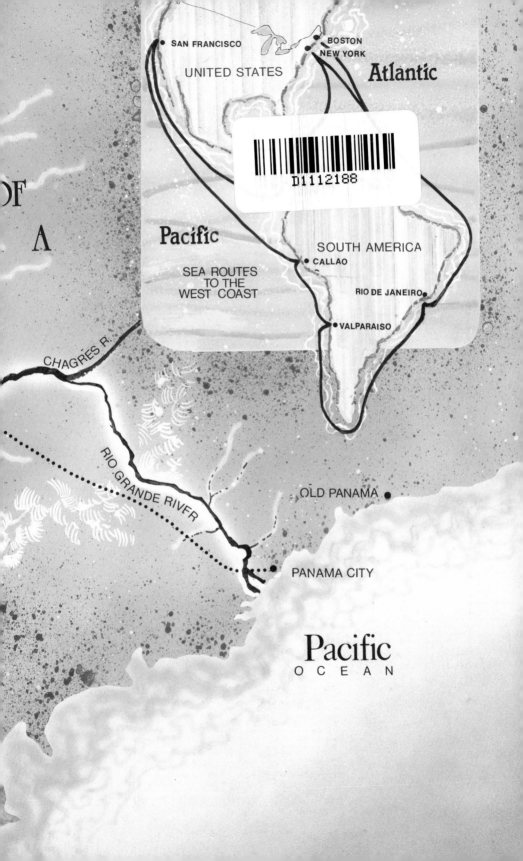

SAN FRANCISCO

BOSTON
NEW YORK

UNITED STATES

Atlantic

OF

A

Pacific

SOUTH AMERICA

CALLAO

SEA ROUTES
TO THE
WEST COAST

RIO DE JANEIRO

VALPARAISO

CHAGRES R.

RIO GRANDE RIVER

OLD PANAMA

PANAMA CITY

Pacific
O C E A N

They Came By Way of Panama

They Came By Way of Panama

by Regina V. Phelan

PROSPERITY PRESS
Spokane, WA   1995

LIBRARY OF CONGRESS CATALOG CARD NUMBER 94-80003
ISBN 0-87062-240-4

First edition

The cover illustrations, chapter head drawings
and endpaper map are from the pen of Alfred G. Champy.
The title page photo is of Andrew Weinshank.

Other books in this series:
The Land Known as Alta California
The Conquered Province
Gold Discovered in California
They Came Around the Horn
They Came Overland by Train
The Story Ends Where It Began:
Along El Camino Real

For further information and inquiries:
REGINA V. PHELAN
1002 West Rd.
La Habra, CA 90631

This book is dedicated to
my sister, Anne W. Wills
and her husband
William T. Wills

They Came
By Way of
Panama

Panama Crossing

CHAPTER I

In the fall of 1855, Andrew Weinshank moved his
family from Alabama to California. He planned to
take them through the Isthmus of Panama. It was a
shorter, quicker trip than going around the Horn. It
would cost more, but Andrew could well afford it.
He sold the 160 acres of land he received as part of
his pay for fighting in the Mexican War. With that
money Andrew was able to book passage for himself, his wife and their two children—Caroline,
who was now six years old and little Frank, just
turned two. On the day of sailing, Regina went
aboard, carrying the baby with little Carrie at her
side. Andrew stayed on the dock looking after their
furniture. They had all their worldly goods with

them; there would be no turning back. After the usual delays and scurrying around, they found their quarters and settled in. Finally, the captain gave the order to pull in the line. Under full steam, they got underway.

They followed the Gulf of Mexico, with a stop at Havana, Cuba. When they arrived at the Isthmus of Panama, the ship dropped anchor two miles or so from the town of Chagres. It had taken ten days to make the trip. In the background, high up on a projecting rock, was the ancient Fort of Chagres. Ahead were seventy-five miles of river and mountain climbing. They stayed on board that night.

The next morning, by rope ladder and sling, the passengers were landed, along with the freight. Each passenger had to sort out his own baggage from the pile which had been dumped on the beach. The furniture stayed aboard. Their ship was to continue on, following the coastline of South America, around the Horn and on to California. The Weinshank's furniture would be stored in a warehouse near the wharf in San Francisco.

The town, located on the Chagres River, was made up of many single-room, grass and bamboo huts with roofs thatched with palmetto leaves. Barking dogs and squealing pigs were running around. The passengers stood by, watching the barefoot men dressed in soiled white trousers and the cigar-smoking women milling around in the crowd. It was the most filthy place imaginable, with garbage in the streets and the flies were everywhere. On the left bank were white frame houses being used as hotels and above them on the bluff was the abandoned castle of San Lorenzo.

The boatman, a padrone as he called himself, was dressed in a muslin shirt, dirty white pants and a large Panama hat. He was smoking a large cigar in his still larger mouth. After agreeing on a price, the passengers made preparations to board his boat. It was a large hollowed-out log, called a bango.

As they got into the bango, all was excitement, for some had misplaced their baggage among the others on the landing. After getting everything straightened out, they were of good cheer and, with a sense of adventure, ready to head up the river. There were no seats in the bango, so, everyone had to sit on their own luggage. The Weinshanks spread out their feather tick, a large sack filled with goose feathers which Regina had brought along, thinking her family might have a use for it.

The padrone took his own jolly good time to get under way. Finally, to the shock of the ladies, off came his Panama hat, his shirt and pants, leaving only his loin cloth. Nothing was said, for the travelers were glad to leave that town, with its stench and filth, behind them. The padrone cradled his long pole against his bare shoulders to propel the boat, keeping it close to shore. At times he would swim ashore with a line and tow the boat from along the riverbank. On occasion, he jumped into the water, seized the gunwales and dragged his boat ahead. Arriving at the most dangerous part of the rapids, the boatman had to exert all his skill and dexterity to keep his boat from dashing against the rocks. It was here the passengers saw many remnants of shattered boats, giving them great concern.

All of a sudden, their bango slapped the water with great force, drenching the passengers. Then, as suddenly as it began, it was all over. Everyone was able to calm down and were grateful for their safety. The ladies fussed with their hair and smoothed out their dresses. When they got to calmer water the padrone spent most of his time resting wherever a patch of shade presented itself.

When their bango came upon the plain, all around were sugar plantations, rice paddies, fields of corn and grazing cattle. As their journey lengthened, the bango became uncomfortable and the heat intense. Sweat ran down their faces. The ladies' hair fell in disarray causing them to wave their fans furiously. The rattling of the tattered awning became a distraction. It was of little use, for it was poor protection against the sun.

From time to time, when it got too hot, the padrone slowed the bango and jumped into the water for a swim, having no consideration for his passengers. After he cooled off, he pulled himself back into the boat and continued on. As the boatman poled slowly along, the air became heavy and the odor intense. The heat became unbearably oppressive. Trees flourished wherever they could get a foothold along the shore. Monkeys chattered in the trees as parrots and water fowl darted along the water's edge, dipping and shrieking. Alligators slid off the mud banks and disappeared into the water with hardly a ripple. This frightened the children, so their father held them tightly.

Every living thing clung and intertwined itself into the various trees along the way. Along either side of the river were rich, bright green, parasitic plants covered with flowers of every hue in the spectrum. In the water were patches of water lilies.

They spent the night at the water's edge. Some brave souls ventured to sleep in the huts along the way, but the Weinshanks preferred to lay out their feather tick in the boat and make out the best they could.

The next morning the boatman got everything in readiness and they continued on their way. It was another day on the river and another night before they arrived at Gorgona. Regina brought out some jerky, dried apples, apricots and molasses from her store of food to feed her family. It was simple but life-sustaining and it would get them by until they could purchase fresh meat and vegetables.

The next town, Cruces, was a little hamlet of thatched palm huts. From there they traveled overland. Andrew hired a donkey for them to continue on to Panama. He threw their feather tick over the beast and helped his wife and children on. At first, the critter wouldn't budge. Andrew first pulled and then pushed him. Regina leaned over, patted him on the neck and he started out. Andrew took the rope leading the donkey and continued on foot. They traveled over a road which was in poor condition with many deep ruts. They spent the night alongside the road.

The next day they had a high mountain to climb. Their donkey made his way steadily up, crossing streams and stumbling over fallen trees that blocked their path. They continued on through a tropical forest with lightning, thunder and incessant rain. They traveled over a cobblestone path so narrow they had to stop and move off to the side to allow an approaching mule train to pass.

The descent was more arduous than the climb. Step by step they made their way down the path constructed of rocks placed in steps by the early Spaniards. This was the same road over which precious gems had been taken out of Mexico to be sent to the Gulf. From there the gems went on to Spain by ship. Native men passed, on their way to Chagres, carrying produce strapped to their heads. Finally, the mountains gave way to the tablelands and in the distance was the welcome sight of Panama.

At length they reached the coastal plains and looked upon the tiled roofs, bell towers and blue waters of the Pacific. As they approached the city of Panama, the country became flat with no trees or vegetation to protect them from the sun. The city before them was a vista of signboards. Panama was an imposing city, with the American flag in evidence everywhere. It was situated on a rocky promontory jutting out into the placid bay. Panama's massive fortifications and many of its buildings were two stories or more in height and many had been built of stone or adobe.

Arriving in the city, the weary travelers tramped over the cobblestones looking for rooms and supplies to replace the things they had lost, broken or consumed along the way. After setting up camp on the outskirts of town, Andrew found a market nearby. There he was able to purchase the first fresh fruit his family had eaten in several days.

When the day came for the Weinshank's to depart the city of Panama, the family assembled on the beach below the sea wall. One by one, first Regina, then Carrie and Andrew carrying Frank, climbed onto the bare shoulders of the native porters and were carried through the breakers to a waiting boat, which took them out to the ship.

Hanging of Cora & Casey

CHAPTER II

On board ship, the passengers were crowded into every available space. Even so, the gentle breezes of the Pacific were a pleasant contrast to the hot, humid climate of Panama. After departing that ancient city, they followed the coastline of Central America on a northerly course. Once the ship crossed the mouth of the Gulf of California, there was more wind and rougher seas. All the next day, the volcano, Colima, a massive peak with clouds curling above its summit, was in sight—a good 140 miles away.

Their ship called at Acapulco. Its harbor, hemmed in by the nearby hills, was a beautiful sight. Since there were no wharves, the ship anchored in the bay and took on sacks of coal, cattle, and an ample supply of food and other provisions. The Weinshanks went ashore to spend the night. In town were many adobe buildings and a beautiful fort built of white sandstone. The fort appeared to be capable of destroying any enemy force that would enter the harbor. It was hot in the town plaza, filled with natives selling fruit, shells and liquor. The Weinshanks walked through the spacious park, purchased some delicious fruits and nuts, then checked into a hotel for a good night's rest. The next day, Regina was reluctant to leave that beautiful spot. However, there was a schedule to keep, so they returned to their ship.

The trip north was a succession of warm days with fair winds, sparkling seas and occasional showers. Spray and waves often swept the deck. Meals consisted of coffee, hard bread and molasses for breakfast, salt pork or corned beef and beans for dinner and hard bread and sugar for supper. For the next few days the shoreline was desolate and barren.

Then, finally, they sailed through the Golden Gate, a narrow strait between two rocks, then into the bay itself. In the distance, silhouetted against the dark hillside, was a cluster of buildings.

Before them were the dusty California hills, large brick buildings, gray tents and dusty shacks on the edge of town, all blending with the chaparral and

dirt of the hills. Their ship pulled in amidst a forest
of masts of whalers and China clippers. Anchored
alongside were steamers and lumber barges from
all corners of the earth. All along the shoreline were
rows of long, narrow wharves extending far into the
bay on pilings. The town itself was built on a gentle
slope.

Andrew went in search of his former commander, Persifer Smith. He had suggested that Andrew
bring his family to California. As commander of
the Pacific Coast, Smith promised Andrew a posi-
tion in his office. Andrew learned General Smith
had been re-assigned and left California. Andrew
would now have to find other employment.

By the time the Weinshanks arrived in San Francisco, gambling had already been outlawed. Now
gamblers were very unpopular. The most hated
man in town was Charlie Cora. He was the owner
of the biggest, fanciest and busiest gambling estab-
lishment in town, El Dorado. But in spite of this,
many a gambler relaxed in the lobby of his saloon.
It was the only place in town where a man could get
in out of the rain, have a bite to eat at his free lunch
counter and transact a little "business" on the side.

Cora, a man of less than medium height, was
dark complected, with large eyes and a black mustache. He always dressed immaculately, wearing a
diamond pin in his cravat. Cora's woman, (for they
had never married) was slight of build, above

medium height. Her skin was as delicately tinted as the pink blossoms on a peach tree.

They attended the American Theatre on the evening of November 15, 1855. Belle was the best-dressed woman in the house that night. She felt perfectly at home in the red plush seats in the first balcony, watching the performance of "Nicodemus." Sitting a few rows in front of them was Mrs. Richardson, wife of the United States Marshal for that district. It was her opinion the likes of Belle should either sit in the seats behind the balcony or in the proscenium boxes. The Marshal walked back to where Cora and Belle were sitting and ordered them to leave. When they refused, he went back to his seat, spoke to his wife and they left.

The next afternoon the Marshal was in the Blue Wing Saloon talking to the bartender when Charlie Cora walked in. The two men greeted each other, had a drink, then walked out together. They started down the street. Suddenly, a shot rang out. Marshal Richardson fell, dead, to the ground. Cora was hustled off to jail. Instantly, there was an epidemic of civic virtue. A vigilante committee gathered to do something about Cora. Some folks thought that had it been the other way around, they would have thought of some way to let him off.

Cora's first trial resulted in a hung jury. He was still sitting in jail, awaiting a second trial. The priest visited Charlie while he was in jail and decided to make an "honest man" of him. He convinced Charlie to marry Belle. The priest performed the ceremony in Cora's cell.

There was another fellow in town by the name of Casey, a young man of 28. Casey was a political power, expert ballot box stuffer, and a desperate fighting man. For reasons unknown to others, Casey decided to lie low for James King of William, editor of the newspaper, the Bulletin. As James King of William was walking down the street, Casey shot James King of William, only wounding him. Casey was arrested and put in jail with Cora.

Later, when the townsfolk learned that James King of William had died, the angry mob again assembled. There were few people on the streets on Sunday, so the Vigilante Committee chose that day to move. Heading toward the jail, the members struck from all directions, approaching on horseback, their glistening bayonets fixed. They placed a brass six-pounder in front of the jail house door and demanded that Casey and Cora be handed over to them. They took their two prisoners to Fort Gunnysack in carriages and tried them before a small crowd on the court house steps. Both men pleaded self-defense. Both men were found guilty of murder.

The funeral for James King of William was held on May 22. Throngs of people crowded the streets in all the available spots along the route. They hung from balconies, clung from windows and sprawled on hilltops along Stockton, Montgomery and Bush Streets. It was the main event of the day. The Weinshanks and their children were there, too.

The crowd moved in the direction of Fort Gunnysack. There a platform had been erected. A man running past the Weinshanks turned and yelled, "You'd better hurry or they'll be hanging Cora and Casey before you get there!"

High above the crowd, the vigilantes pushed both men onto the platform. A white cloth covered their heads and was tied down around their necks. Their arms were tied down to their sides and their feet were bound. In his hand Cora held a handkerchief. He remained silent. Casey wanted to speak his piece, so a man stepped up and removed his cover. While he was talking, the Weinshanks were being pushed along with the crowd and were within the sound of his voice.

Neither Regina nor Andrew wanted their children to watch the hangings so they turned to leave. As they were walking away Andrew looked back. He saw them again cover Casey's head. The platform was then pulled out from under the two men, leaving them swinging in mid-air. Cora's handkerchief went fluttering to the ground! Later, Belle took Charlie's body to Mission Dolores. There, he was buried in the courtyard.

Pueblo de Los Angeles

CHAPTER III

Andrew got an order to make barrels for the miners of the territory. This meant his family would be moving to the Pueblo de Los Angeles, a small Mexican village in the southern part of the state. Andrew was to make the barrels and Regina would fill them with foodstuffs. Her recipes were used at the family restaurant at Monte Carlo in the south of France. Their contract called for catsup, pickled turnips and sauerkraut. They considered themselves fortunate, for they had a market for their products. As soon as their contract was signed, sealed and delivered, they made plans to move to El Pueblo de Los Angeles.

There was a great hubbub on the wharf in San

Francisco, as the sidewheeler, the *Ohio*, was about to head on down the coast. The Weinshank children, Carrie and little Frank took in everything there was to see. They walked up the gangplank of the long, sleek, majestic sidewheeler. Her upper deck was topped by a lofty, black stack. Her white paint glistened in the bright sunlight and her flag, stirred by a mild breeze, fluttered lazily overhead. The Weinshanks stayed on deck as they left the harbor and watched the paddles churn the water into a frothing foam. After a short but pleasant voyage the town of Monterey burst into view. Above it loomed the rolling mesa, mantled in emerald green, with pine-covered hills beyond. Before them, in a large quadrangle, stood the Presidio buildings with an imposing chapel dome towering above the walled-in enclosure. To their right lay the anchorage. From the deck they could see a few houses with white-washed walls and red tiled roofs scattered over the grassy plains.

The next day, the *Ohio* continued on down the coast and dropped anchor in the bay of Santa Barbara. As the ship entered the harbor, the Weinshanks, again watching from the deck, could see a scattering of white-washed adobes with red tile roofs clustered inside the crumbling walls of the plaza. They saw men on horseback riding on the beach with their families lumbering along behind, in carretas.

Since there was no wharf the passengers and freight were taken ashore in small boats. Andrew and Regina, holding onto their little ones, looked on anxiously, waiting to see if the passengers would make it without serious mishaps. Suddenly, a boat capsized and emptied its occupants into the water, much to the amusement of those on board the sidewheeler. As the boats approached shallow water, the passengers and their baggage were carried to dry land by the sailors. After the people had been delivered to the shore and the sailors returned to the ship, the sidewheeler continued on.

As the *Ohio* approached the harbor of the Pueblo de Los Angeles on that beautiful spring day, the Weinshanks were startled by the sound of the signal gun. The crew readied the small craft for the passengers to go ashore. First the ladies and children, followed by the men. When they reached shallow water, they were carried ashore by the sailors.

They saw no buildings, just flat, open space. Standing by a wagon on the beach was a big, powerful man. His brightly-colored suspenders added to the picturesque effect of his costume. His pantaloons were short, his socks holey, and shoes crude. Both coatless and vestless, he wore neither necktie nor collar.

He directed the passengers to his nearby wagon, waiting to take them into town. It was the common, western variety with four rows of four seats pulled by six horses in primitive harness. The front row included the driver, Sam Jones, a big man with scraggly beard and piercing eyes. He was known by the townsfolk as "Jonesy." Regina got in and sat by him, then the children squeezed in, leaving Andrew on the outside. Andrew gave Jonesy a five dollar bill for the fare. When all the seats were filled, not a minute was lost. Jonesy cracked his whip, called out to his team and they were away at a breakneck speed.

Jonesy leaned over and yelled at Andrew, "Banning was the man who greeted you on shore. He can drive a six-horse rig faster, over rougher roads than anyone who ever cracked the whip or pulled the ribbons."

"Sounds like quite a man," Andrew replied.

"Last year Banning and some other fellows bought fifteen wagons and one hundred fifty mules. They transported goods from the harbor. They traveled over the Old Spanish Trail, then on to the Mormon settlement at Salt Lake in the Utah territory. They left El Monte, near the San Gabriel Mission, in early May and traveled through open cattle range to the Mormon settlement in San Bernardino. It's at the bottom of that range of mountains," said Jonesy, pointing it out. "They held up there, waited for the winter snows to melt over the pass and didn't return until September."

"I've never seen so much open space in all my born days," commented Regina.

They saw cattle grazing over the countryside as they continued on, traveling through Rancho San Pedro. Jonesy liked having a couple of greenhorns at his side.

On either side of the road were fences covered with strings of hide drying in the sun. On the ranchos, the hides were used to make latch strings, hinges, shoe laces, mats, woven chair seats, lariats, bedsteads and rope for wooden plows and ox carts.

On the many ranchos in the valley, each ranchero was "lord and master" over his big family and his poor relations. Living on his rancho were harness makers, wool combers, tanners, carpenters and many Indian vaqueros and servants. Their adobes consisted mostly of bedrooms. The cooking was done outside. Their beds were made of cowhide fastened to a frame with four legs. They were alive with fleas, as were the hides that were strewn around the room. The little "malditos," as they called them, were crawling out of the cracks of the walls.

"Work on the ranchos is all done by the Indians. They make the adobe bricks, plant the corn, crush the grapes, grind the wheat into flour, bake the bread, cradle the babies and haul the hides to market," explained Jonesy.

"What would happen to this country if they didn't have the Indians to do all the work?" asked Regina.

"You got me!" answered Jonesy.

He came to a skidding halt at the half-way house to change horses. The Weinshanks, along with the other passengers, had a chance to get a bite to eat before continuing on.

Back on the trail, they passed several roads coming in from the ranchos. The roads came in from all directions, like the spokes of a lopsided wheel. The roads came in from the vineyards and cornfields, from the ocean or the mountains, from Mission San Gabriel, from the tar pits, from Mission San Fernando, from Campo Santo Cemetery on Eternity Street, from Santa Barbara and from Redondo, where salt was available. When a pack train caravan loaded down with goods came in from Santa Fe, New Mexico, they came by the King's Highway, the most important highway of all: El Camino Real.

The rancheros came to town to make cattle deals, buy liquor, saddles or supplies, watch the horse races, play a little monte or drop by the corral and see a bear or bull fight. Some times they came to arrange a baptism, a wedding or a funeral.

After traveling the twenty-seven miles over the mesa at a goodly clip, their wagon turned onto San Pedro Street, a narrow lane no wider than needed to pass another stage or wagon. The roadway was lined with willows. The nearby fields were planted to grapes. Carrie covered her ears, cutting out the noise of shouts and yells as Jonesy was hailed by every inhabitant and dog along the way.

At last, Jonesy pulled up at the Bella Union Hotel, a single-story adobe on the corner of Main and Commercial Streets. Andrew helped Regina and the children down and grabbed their suitcases. As they entered the hotel, they were greeted by the manager standing behind the counter. It was Dr. Hammel, a small, energetic man. Not giving Andrew a chance to put down his bags, he ushered them out the back door of the hotel to one of the rooms out back. It was a small room, scarcely six feet by nine, with a low ceiling and a dirt floor. There was hardly enough room for their bed and baggage. There they would stay until they could find a place of their own.

While the children were napping, Regina and Andrew unpacked their belongings and tidied up a bit. After the Weinshanks had a bite to eat, Dr. Hammel offered to show them around the Plaza, just a few doors down the street, the center of town.

On the streets everyone was on the move, with jingling spurs, cavorting steeds and whizzing riatas. It was a rip-roaring town with many saloons and gambling houses. All around were adobes. Toward the north was a single pepper tree providing the only shade in town. Nearby was a stone reservoir. They stopped to look at the other buildings facing the Plaza. The church, Our Lady, Queen of the Angels, faced the large corral-like Plaza.

They walked along slowly, passing Don Ygnacio Del Valle's adobe on the east side of the square, between Calle de Los Negroes and Vine Street. Valle, the Alcalde, was known about town as a man of culture and refinement. He operated the only public school in town. The City Council was paying Valle fifteen dollars a month to instruct classes in his home. He had served as a Captain under General Flores when the Californians fought against Fremont at Cahuenga. It was Valle's job to record the brands, grants and other property transactions. Across from him, on the other side of the street, lived Don Augustin Olvera.

They stopped to admire Don Vicente Lugo's adobe. He was killed in the battle of Paso de Bartola near the Rio Hondo River. While taking everything in, Dr. Hammel pointed out the beautiful two-story adobe belonging to Vicente Sanchez. They continued on, passing a group of Indians sitting on the ground, the sun beating down on them.

Dr. Hammel was enjoying his role as guide, telling them all about the town and its people. "When the senoritas come to town to shop, they want wood sidewalks to keep their sweeping skirts from getting dirty. They don't like walking in the mud in the winter and the dust in the summer. The women-folk not only fuss about the sidewalks, but about the tar dripping down from the rooftops. They are trying to get a law passed to force the shop owners to fix their roofs. The women also insist on hitching posts being put up to keep the rancheros from taking lead ropes into the stores."

"Sometimes it takes the women to get things done," replied Regina. Andrew frowned.

As they walked along on the dirt road, caballeros, ten abreast, their saddles adorned with silver, came riding down the street. The riders were wearing fine Panama hats, tightly fitted jackets of brightly colored material of blue, green and yellow, trimmed in gold and silver fringe and matching pantaloons. The Weinshanks applauded the caballeros as they passed by. Others on the street joined in the applause.

Passing by were carretas laden down with hides, pulled slowly along by plodding oxen, wheels creaking, stirring up the dust. Several of the men in town were dealing in hides and had a good trade. They stored them in a warehouse until they accumulated a goodly number, then took them by carreta to the ships waiting in the harbor. It was the biggest business in town. The children became restless, so Doctor Hammel and the Weinshanks started back to the hotel.

San Gabriel Mission

CHAPTER IV

Andrew moved his family into their new adobe at 744 Fort Street, a narrow, dirt lane with a few one-story adobes scattered around. Along the front of the adobe was a veranda with a flat roof supported by four posts. Andrew tried the hand-hewn door and found it to be open. They walked into the barren room with thick, white-washed walls. In the corner of the sala (living room), on the earthen floor, was a brasero, a pan used for holding hot coals for heating. Off the sala were two small bedrooms. There was no kitchen, for the cooking was to be done outside.

Soon after they moved in, they received word their furniture had arrived from San Francisco. Andrew found Captain Salisbury Haley of the *Ohio* at the Bella Union Hotel, his favorite haunt, playing cards in the dining room.

The next morning the Captain and Andrew went by carreta to the harbor. There the sidewheeler, with the furniture aboard, was anchored off-shore. The furniture was on deck when they arrived. The sailors let each piece down by rope, to the waiting flat boat, then floated it into shore. After everything was loaded into the waiting carreta, Andrew jumped in and made himself as comfortable as possible. The driver walked along side, keeping the oxen to the road. It was a slow and bumpy ride over the twenty-seven miles back to Los Angeles. Andrew, along with his furniture got a good jostling around.

While the Weinshanks were unloading their furniture, a rickety wagon, loaded with barrels, drawn by two broken-down horses, pulled up to their door. The driver, a tall red-headed American with a bushy mustache, wearing long rubber boots, introduced himself as Bill, the water man. He gave them a helping hand carrying their furniture into the house. Later, he explained, "1 will deliver all the water you can drink for fifty cents a week." Andrew nodded his head in agreement and Bill placed a large jug, an urn-shaped vessel of burnt clay, on the veranda. The water came from the Los Angeles River. This was the same place where the ladies did their washing, the townspeople dumped their garbage and the children bathed. The town council prohibited it, but no one paid any heed.

Out back, Andrew and Regina unpacked their kettles and barrels and got down to work. Much had to be done. Regina gathered her spices together and arranged them on the table. Andrew left the house in search of cabbage, tomatoes and cucumbers. He made his first stop at the "Montgomery," a well-known gambling house located near Stearn's "El Palacio," run by Billy Getman. The "Montgomery" was a long building, fronted with a veranda, facing Calle Principal. From the Montgomery, Andrew went to the heart of the business section between Main and Spring Streets, to John G. Downey's drug store. As he crossed the road, a wagon load of ice passed by, going in the direction of Sonora Town. As he walked along the plank sidewalk under the veranda, he could feel the vibration of some local urchins running foot races over his head.

He passed a man pushing a wheelbarrow, stopping whenever a customer appeared. Andrew stopped and looked over his produce, "Quite a cart you have here."

"It'll do," the man replied.

"My name is Andrew Weinshank. I guess we're in the same business."

"Free country. Suit yourself. I'm Andy Briswalter. I grow everything here in my backyard."

"Maybe we can buy from you. We'll need tomatoes, cucumbers and turnips."

"Yes, I grow those. Let me know what you need, and we'll try to work something out."

"I'll do that."

Coming towards him was a Mexican woman peddling huevos (eggs) in a pan. Andrew's last stop was the Bella Union Hotel, hoping to get an order from them, then on home. When Andrew returned home after making his purchases and getting orders for their products, their Indian helpers, Jesse and Arturo, set about getting the fire started. Regina started preparing the day's supply of foodstuffs for the market.

One pleasant spring day, the Weinshanks and their friends the Childs rode out into the country. They went by way of Aliso Street, which narrowed to a picturesque little lane. In the back of the wagon, the children talked and laughed as they rode along on their way to the Mission San Gabriel Archangel. They crossed a slow-moving stream and headed for the open country. There were sycamore and oak trees here and there and willows along the riverbanks and country lanes. They traveled through meadows of wild mustard growing in great profusion. Bees moved busily among the wildflowers.

The children were excited as they rode along, for

they knew they would be getting treats. They would have a chance to play in the room where the branding irons were stored and look down into the pits where tallow was rendered in the old days.

As they neared the mission, they drove through lands covered with vineyards in every direction. At last they saw the Mission ahead of them. Entering the grounds, they saw the ruins of the surrounding adobes, where once had been a good sized town. An immense amount of labor had been wrought upon this lovely valley making it into a paradise. Now, only a few tall date palms were standing. The grounds were desolate and overgrown with weeds. The whole area had reverted back to its once desert-like condition. The church itself showed signs of decay but was still very much intact. The outer buildings showed little evidence of their former walls.

They hitched their wagon to a post and were warmly greeted by a priest. An Indian helper took the children off to the cook house while the grown-ups talked and looked around. The padre related the sad story of the decline of the mission, "In this land of abundance you would think we had not a care in the world, but without our Indian help, we can no longer tend to our orchards and fields. Most of the land has been taken from us, our vines are dying, and we have no money to pay for help"

"That is very sad indeed," said Emmalina, as

they continued their stroll about the grounds. Later, they walked into the courtyard where the graveyard was. The padre showed them where as many as fourteen Indians had been buried in a single grave. The Indians had caught the white man's diseases and died by the score.

In the garden, the orange trees were so heavily laden with fruit, the branches were propped up so they would not break. While Andrew and Ozro were filling their bags with oranges, Regina and Emmalina went in search of the children. They found them in the cook house and brought them back to the wagon. It was time for them to leave. The children, all bundled up, were sound asleep when they arrived home.

Ozro Childs

CHAPTER V

It was wash day at the Pueblo de Los Angeles. The Weinshanks and Childs went down to the river to do their laundry. Regina wanted to wash her curtains so they would be fresh for Christmas. She was careful to place her scrub board on the outer edge of the canal so her dirty water would not mix with the water intended for drinking purposes. She spread out their clothes on the rocks to dry, and the ladies sat down to chat. Wash days were fun because Carrie was with her best friend, Emma. With little Frank tagging along, they all went off to play. Later in the afternoon, the men folk joined them.

Ozro was the talkative one. He told them that when gold was first discovered, Hugo Reid went to the gold fields to check things over. Reid wrote to Don Abel Stearns in Los Angeles that there was a need for fresh meat in San Francisco. He suggested the rancheros herd their cattle north.

Huge herds, often numbering in the thousands, were driven hundreds of miles to San Francisco, taking over a month to make the trip. At nightfall the vaqueros would set up camp, cut out a steer from the herd, lasso and butcher it, barbecue what they needed and leave the rest to rot. Bones and skulls could be seen all along the trail from the Pueblo de Los Angeles to San Francisco. Sometimes some of the stock was lost in the tall fields of mustard because of the heavy fog. The vaqueros would waste time looking for them. Occasionally they herded the stock through poisonous weeds. When they neared the gold fields, they grazed their cattle on the outskirts of town to fatten them up. Prices went soaring up from five dollars a head to thirty dollars, or more. At one time beef got up to a dollar a pound.

As Ozro continued to tell them about the early days in the Pueblo, Emma overheard her father talking about the famous horse race that took place the year before. She wanted Carrie and Frank to hear it too, so the three small children sat down at Ozro's feet to listen.

One horse, Sarco, belonged to Don Pio Pico and the other, Black Swan, belonged to Don Jose Sepul-

veda. People came from as far away as San Francisco and San Diego to place their bets and watch
the race. Starting at San Pedro Street, they were to
circle a post four and one-half miles away and
return to town.

Each man thought his horse would win the
twenty-five thousand dollars in gold plus five hundred head each of mares, calves and sheep put up
by the loser. The wager was written up, witnessed
and made legal. Don Pio Pico's horse, Sarco, was
well-known to be the best and fastest in all California. Don Jose Sepulveda brought Black Swan all the
way from Australia. Pico had a local Mexican as his
rider, but Sepulveda wouldn't say who his rider
was.

On the day of the big race, the streets in town were
crowded with people mingling in wild confusion.
Nothing of such importance had ever happened in
their town before. Members of both the Pico and
Sepulveda households passed out gold pieces so
their servants could bet on their owner's horse.

When the race was about to begin, both horses
were led to the starting place. The Mexican rider
mounted Sarco. Then a Negro boy, dressed in a
fancy outfit, appeared. The crowd noticed he wasn't
a boy at all, but a very small man. He was using a
light-weight English type saddle. With the starting
signal they were off at full tilt. They reached the
half-way post together, but Black Swan pulled out

ahead in the final stretch. The lightweight saddle and experienced rider made the difference.

Ozro told them about Don Abel Stearns. He was one of the first white men to come to the Pueblo. He came in 1829. He traded hides and tallow with the sailors on the ships anchored in the harbor. With the profits from his business, he purchased tens of thousands of acres of land. He purchased his twenty-seven-thousand-acre Los Cerritos Rancho from one of the Nieto heirs. He became good friends with Don Juan Bandini, the great ranchero in San Diego. Don Abel Stearns fell in love with Bandini's beautiful daughter, Arcadia. Her father approved of the marriage, even though Stearns was foreign-born and forty-three years old at the time. Arcadia was only fourteen.

The Stearn's parties were grand affairs. Their hospitality could not be equaled anywhere else in the country. They had only to pass the word and everyone joined in the fiesta. The wealthy Don Pio Pico came into town from his "El Ranchito" across the mesa to attend Don Abel's fandangos.

Sometimes Don Bandini, Don Coronel and Don Andres Pico would get together and rent a hall. Everyone bought a ticket for the dance. The money was given to charity. Solomon Lazard was the floor manager at the balls and fandangos. Long tables of food were set up. The townsfolk danced to the sweet strains of the guitar and violin far into the night. For those who didn't dance, it was great fun anyway just watching the beautiful senoritas as they danced with their handsome caballeros. The only lights shining in town were those in the building where the dance was being held, otherwise, all was in total darkness.

Just then Andrew felt a drop of rain, then another. As it began to rain harder, the Weinshanks and the Childs hurriedly collected their belongings and put them into the wagon. After gathering up the children, they quickly headed for home.

It rained all that night and the next day. By late in the afternoon their roof began to leak. Regina went looking for Andrew and found him working in the shed.

"The roof is leaking, Andrew."

"I'll do something about it right away." Regina went back to the house. She no sooner got in than it started raining even harder, coming down in "buckets." Andrew's work would have to wait. He had been attaching a tree limb to a log making a chauncer to press sauerkraut into the barrel.

Andrew went to Calle de Los Negroes. After talking to several men who were standing around, he learned that Vicente Salcido was the only man in town who repaired roofs. He found Salcido's house easily enough because of the many barrels he kept in his front yard. Andrew was lucky to find him home, catching him before he got too busy with the on-coming of the rainy season. After the two men decided on a price, Vicente assured him he would be there as soon as possible.

A few days later, Andrew heard a racket outdoors and went to check it out. He found Vicente setting up his kettle in the middle of the road, directly in front of their house. He had already begun to build a fire under it. While the tar was heating, Vicente climbed up onto the roof and cleaned it off. He then went back to the kettle and threw in some pitch. Next, he hauled the melted tar up onto the roof in buckets and spread it over the leaky roof. After that was done, the Weinshanks felt much better, knowing their roof was fixed.

Even though the rain caused a great deal of damage, it was important to everyone. When the rain fell, the stock flourished and everybody thrived. When they had dry years, cattle and horses perished and everyone's pocketbooks remained empty. The rain meant the difference between success and failure. Every day Andrew and Regina looked to the sky for any overhanging clouds, praying for the much needed rain.

Jesse watched the catsup on the stove while Regina and Arturo kept busy shredding cabbage for the sauerkraut. Andrew had his hands full just making barrels.

He worked out back in the shed, spending hours sanding the barrels on the inside until they were as smooth as glass. He used brass hoops from his friend, Ozro Childs' tin shop to keep the staves tight. While he was busy working, he listened for the squeaking sound of the carretas in the distance. He knew they would be bringing women and children. The women would be buying their foodstuffs. The carretas would be followed by howling dogs, and alongside would be a handsome caballero on horseback, prodding his wandering oxen, holding them to the road.

This would give them time to get everything ready. Jesse and Regina were inside while Andrew was helping Arturo get their products lined up for the ladies to see. When the carreta pulled up in front of their adobe, its occupants all climbed out. The ladies entered the house, smelled the good aromas, sniffed the sauerkraut, sipped some of Regina's catsup and tasted her cooked vegetables. They made their purchases, got back into their carretas and went on their way.

After they left, the Weinshanks walked to town. They looked at the rudely lettered signs on the store front, painted on unbleached cloth, advertising wares. Mr. Newmark had one over his. It was around noon. Andrew tried the door. It was open, but no Mr. Newmark.

Andrew remarked, "Oh, I'll bet Harris is off playing cards somewhere."

"Why don't these merchants tend to business? asked Regina. "People expect me to have my food products ready when I say I'll have them."

Then she started looking over his merchandise. She wanted to pick up a few trinkets for the children for Christmas. While she was shopping, Mr. Newmark walked in, "Just talking to some of my neighbors. Can I help you people?"

"We're looking around. I'll let you know what we need."

Mr Newmark turned to Carrie, now seven years old. "This might interest you. A woman came into my store one day. She picked up a pair of shoes, and put them inside her clothes. l walked up to her and said, 'Give them to me!' and she gave them back. She smiled at me just as nice as you please, bowed and walked out of the store."

Regina joined them and said, "I doubt if she ever steals from you again, Mr. Newmark. I hope you don't ever do that, Carrie. I'd like to buy these items, please."

"Thank you, kind lady. Can we just put them in your bag?"

"You certainly may."

Just then, the church bells began to chime, and Mr. Newmark stopped to listen. "Those bells send many a faithful to early mass or announce the time of vespers, and I might add, call many a merchant to his day's labor and dismiss him to his home."

"They have a comforting sound and they're very helpful for us in our work, too."

"I eat in town and have been enjoying some of your handiwork, Regina."

"It's nice of you to say so. Well, it's time to go home, Carrie."

"I hope you will come back soon," said Mr. New-mark.

"We will, thank you and good day."

Regina and Carrie walked over to Mr. Hellman's store. Regina looked up to see a caballero, one she had seen performing in a parade. She noticed he had a reata in his hand. As she walked past, he bowed politely, lowering his reata. She stepped over it and walked into the store. They looked around. On one counter, Carrie saw some books.

"Look at these, mama!"

"Carrie, would you like to borrow one?" asked Mr. Hellman as he walked toward her, smiling.

"Yes, I would Mr. Hellman. Maybe one of the Sisters will help me with it." So with book in hand, she was a happy little girl.

Carrie attended school conducted by the Sisters of Charity. She was one of seven children who attended that year. The Sisters were conducting both the school and an orphanage in one of the first frame buildings in the pueblo. The building was located on Alameda and Macy Streets and had been sold to them by Don Benito Wilson. The school was well run from the start, for Sister Superior had ample funds to manage it. However, the public school did not fare so well. The town council made all the decisions and some of the members felt frills were unnecessary. They refused to hire a janitor. They felt that if the classroom floor needed to be swept, the teacher should appoint a pupil to swing the broom.

Carreta

CHAPTER VI

On January 9, 1857, at half past eight in the morning, the Weinshanks were preparing foodstuffs for the market. The earth began to tremble. Big kettles out back tipped over and barrels fell from the shelves. At first the shocks were light, then stronger. Andrew and Regina quickly gathered up the children and ran outside. Jesse and Arturo ran away. Horses darted in all directions, running at full tilt down Fort Street. Fearful of further shocks, they stayed outside. After a few minutes, when everything quieted down, they went back inside. Jesse and Arturo returned and followed them through the dusty doorway. Everything was in shambles, so they went about setting things straight.

Times became very hard, for it had been a dry season. Even the richest of the rancheros felt the pinch. Many began to part with their lands to secure relief to tide them over.

One day Sheriff James Barton, a big, burly fellow with a bushy mustache, knocked on their door. Regina poured the sheriff and Andrew each a tall glass of cool water and the two men sat down and talked. After a bit Barton got around to telling Andrew the purpose of his visit...taxes. "I'll be happy to pay as soon as we can get our feet on the ground," said Andrew.

"I know you will, Andrew. Just do the best you can." As the sheriff was preparing to leave a man raced up on horseback to tell him Pancho Daniel had broken out of jail and was holing up at San Juan Capistrano. Pancho Daniel and his band of more than a hundred men had already killed a man by the name of George Pfeugardt and were planning to kill more.

The sheriff started giving orders. "Regina, take the children to the Armory. It will be safe there. Andrew, grab your gun and come along with me."

The men hurried off. Regina gathered up the children, a few things they would need and, along with Jesse and Arturo, left for the Armory.

From the jailhouse, Sheriff Barton sent word to the Texas boys in El Monte to join the posse. They were a tough bunch of young men who had fought in the Mexican War. They responded quickly. Before the posse left in search of Pancho Daniel, the sheriff was warned by Don Jose Sepulveda to take more men with him. They were outnumbered two to one. Sheriff Barton disregarded Sepulveda's advice and started out.

The next day they were met by the marauders in Santiago Canyon. In the shoot-out, four men were killed. Sheriff Barton was one of them. When the posse returned to Los Angeles, word spread throughout town. Nearly one hundred armed men left early the next morning to track down the fugitives. Andrew left in a wagon with four coffins to bring back the bodies of Barton and his comrades. Returning the next day, he drove down Main Street. Business was suspended and the townsfolk turned out to follow the coffin-laden wagon to the burial grounds. Don Abel Stearns and his wife, Arcadia, rode up in their stylish carriage. The Gollers drove up in one of their wagons. All the others arrived in carretas or on foot.

After the coffins were lowered into the ground, Regina and the children walked on home, while Andrew returned the wagon to the Gollers. Andres Pico quickly mounted his horse and headed out in the direction of Santiago Canyon.

James Thompson took over Barton's job as sheriff and quickly captured fifty-two of the culprits and brought them back for quick "justice." Judge Scott presided. He wanted to get it over with. The Wein-shanks were there watching the proceedings. The prisoners, one after another, were brought before the judge, who then called upon the crowd to determine their fate. Someone yelled out, "Hang him!" and the Judge responded by saying, "You've heard the motion. All those in favor, signify by saying 'aye.'" And, of course, the "ayes" had it.

After the verdict was rendered, some of the men in the posse went to the jailhouse. They subdued the jailer, Frank Carpenter, because he refused to surrender the prisoners. After getting the prisoners out of jail, they took them to the gallows next to the school yard on Fort Street. In front of every man, woman and child in the pueblo, they strung them up, one at a time. For a while the children had the best spot of all. They watched the whole proceeding through the peep holes in the board fence on the school yard. Someone in the crowd spotted them and shouted, "Hey, look at them kids watching!" Judge Scott quickly hustled them off to their homes.

Bucket Brigade

CHAPTER VII

Andrew Weinshank went to Joseph Downey's drugstore to put some of his hard-earned money in Downey's safe. He walked in the door holding up his bag. "How about it, Joe? Can I put this money in your safe?"

"You certainly can, Andrew. Come in any time and pick it up."

"Much obliged," said Andrew as he put the bag of money on the counter.

As Andrew was walking out the door, he heard the sound of rapid pistol shots, the signal for a fire. He quickly headed in that direction. The fire was in his friend Ozro Childs' tin shop. The bucket-brigade had already formed a relay from the zanja (ditch). The buckets were being passed briskly along from one person to the next. The flames were spreading rapidly. Both the Bella Union and El Palacio were being threatened. By the time Andrew arrived, almost everyone in town was there watching, including his own two children. When the fire was finally brought under control, someone in the crowd remarked, "We need one of those fancy fire engines like the one they have in San Francisco."

When Andrew found Ozro, he was sitting on a crate, head in hand, bemoaning his losses. Andrew went over to him, patted him on the back and the two men got to work cleaning up the debris.

Most men wore guns and some felt they had to use them. One day, Andrew's friend, Gabe Allen, a Mexican War veteran was walking down Calle de Los Negroes. He saw a man on a rooftop and took aim at him. Sheriff Billy Rowland was standing nearby and saw Gabe. He was able to knock Gabe down before he could get his shot off. The Sheriff could tell Gabe had been drinking, so he hauled him off to jail. Andrew passed them as they were walking along. Seeing the sheriff had the reeling Gabe under control, he decided to leave well enough alone. From there, Andrew went over to the Temple block. Daniel Desmond, the hatter was renting one of Temple's stores. Andrew saw a new "stove pipe" hat displayed in Desmond's window. He thought it quite handsome. He walked into the store. While he was looking at the hat, Mr. Desmond stepped up.

"How do you like that hat, Andrew?"

"Very nice," he answered.

"The Congressman from Illinois, Abe Lincoln, wears one just like it. This is the hat that replaced the beaver. Beaver, you know is getting scarce; very few are even being made these days." Andrew stood there a while and admired it. He tried it on and was impressed. Before he had a chance to change his mind and feeling a little flush for having money in Downey's safe, he decided to buy it. He then went on home.

Bella Union Hotel

CHAPTER VIII

The Pueblo de Los Angeles was a rip-roaring town. Nightly shootings kept the pitch of excitement at Calle de Los Negroes at its height. Liquor flowed in abundance and the sound of guitars was heard throughout the Pueblo. The streets were lined with saloons and gambling houses. The town's reputation for violence was unparalleled. Murderers, bandits and thieves were living there. It was best described as a "den of thieves," teeming with the lowest of low life. It was a place for the restless and reckless. The drunkards, the gamblers, and the ruffians were all living there, many having been run out of San Francisco by the vigilantes.

When law and order became somewhat established, the jury system was inaugurated. Those serving conducted themselves rather informally in court. During the warm weather, neither vests nor collars were worn. Each juror provided himself with a stick of wood and a knife in order to whittle away his time, while listening to the case. If, by any chance, he forgot his stick, he whittled on the chair he was sitting on. Andrew was asked to serve, but not knowing the custom, had neither knife nor wood to occupy his time.

Sheriff Rowland, with the recent Gabe Allen incident on his mind, got up before the jury and tried to pass a law to control the indiscriminate firing of pistols. His plea fell on deaf ears. One of the leading citizens on the jury got up and said the judges weren't acting firmly enough in handing down sentences. He felt criminals were being released from jail and allowed to return to the streets to commit crimes over and over again.

One fellow was brought to court, tried and found guilty. When the sheriff discovered the prisoner was his brother-in-law, one he had never met, he convinced the jury to recommend clemency. Judge Dryden, in announcing the verdict, peered over his glasses and said, "The jury finds you guilty as charged." He then proceeded to give the prisoner a lecture, ending with, "I now declare you a free man. You may go about your business." One man in the crowd yelled out, "What's his business,

Judge?" The judge responded, "His 'business,' sir, is horse stealing."

One day while Andrew was serving on the jury, Regina and the children walked into town. As they walked up the steps of the brick building on the corner of Franklin and Spring Streets, Frank yanked at his mother's skirt and pointed, "Golly sakes, look over there. Those men are chained to logs.

"Let them be, Frank. This is the jailhouse, those men are prisoners." Just then, Andrew came out the door.

On the street an impressive figure rode by. It was the great Don Julio Verdugo, himself, mounted on a beautiful horse. He was wearing a low-crowned, wide-brimmed, black hat and had a colorful handkerchief around his neck. It was election day. Following were his son, Victoriano Verdugo, and Victoriano's thirteen sons, all coming to town to vote for their father's favorite candidate. The boys were decked out in their fancy velvet clothes, ornamented with decorative braid and silver buttons flashing in the sunlight. Following closely behind, riding in carretas were other members of the family.

They were heading in the direction of Sonora Town on the other side of the Plaza. That was where the families lived who had come to California from Sonora, Mexico, with Governor Felipe de Neve. They were the first to settle the land. Those first buildings in Los Angeles were now being used as places for drinking.

They were going there to look for men to vote. They would take the men to the corral, offer them as much free liquor as they could drink, put them in one of Phineas Banning's wagons and take them to the voting place. There they were given a ticket to deposit in the ballot box. Since all the influential Mexican candidates were Democrats, they controlled the elections.

It was the white man who brought the Indians down to a state of debauchery. Drunkenness was a curse for the poor Indians, who were sold the cheapest liquor, causing untold misery. Every Saturday night the streets were filled with sodden, drunken wretches lying alongside the road and in the gutters. The sheriff locked up the drunks and buried the dead. On Monday morning, those who had survived were lined up outside the jailhouse and sold to the highest bidder. They were then sent to work on a rancho or in a winery until the following Friday night.

One day Andrew, Regina and the children took a picnic lunch and went to Fort Hill, up above the town where they could look down on the church. Nearby was Vincent Lugo's adobe. Close by was the old Mexican adobe jailhouse, now falling into ruin. Andrew and Regina were enjoying sitting in the shade of the old adobe, looking down on the town and out over the countryside. Vast grazing lands stretched out before them. Many acres were planted to oranges and vineyards grew in every direction. Much of the land belonged to William Wolfskill.

Wolfskill had worked on a schooner fitted out at San Pedro to hunt sea otter and had returned to settle down south of town in 1830. Before that he was a trapper in the territory. Both he and Antonio Maria Lugo set out grapevines. Wolfskill planted his in 1838. He was led to believe his vines would live a hundred years.

"Look down there, Andrew, you can see all the orange trees Mr. Wolfskill has planted, row after row. I've never seen so many in all my born days."

"I had some in Mexico, wonderful tasting," said Andrew.

"We had them in France, too," replied Regina. "How long before they'll bear?"

"Oh, about five years."

"I understand some shade trees are going to be planted at the Plaza."

"We certainly need them," noted Andrew. "We only have that one pepper tree there now."

"Isn't this wonderful, looking down on the town? You once told me that California was heaven on earth. Do you still feel that way, Andrew?"

"Yes, I do. It's just too bad some of those poor

devils down there don't realize how lucky they are to be here. The sky is clear, the mountains are beautiful and the weather is mild," Andrew remarked as he turned his back to the mountains and looked toward the sea.

"It's strange Los Angeles isn't nearer the ocean. They must have had a reason," remarked Regina.

"That river down there is the reason," said Andrew as Regina spread out a blanket and arranged their lunch. Just then, the children came back from their chase through the mustard and they ate a hearty lunch, then went on home.

One day while the Weinshanks were in town, they walked into John Shumacher's grocery store, the busiest place in town. John had come from Germany to this country. He had been in Stevenson's Regiment of New York Volunteers. In 1847, the Volunteers came to San Francisco as guards during the war with Mexico. After his term in the Army, Shumacher settled down at Sutter's Creek to dig for gold. He came to Los Angeles with one nugget in his pocket worth eight hundred dollars, enough to establish himself in business.

While the Weinshanks were looking at his merchandise, John said, "I like dealing with the Mormons because they're so dependable and their vegetables and eggs are always fresh, even if it takes a few days to get here. I'll bet those turnips you're looking at were dug the day before they headed out."

"They are a hard-working people, all right."

"Yes, and good businessmen."

"They're bound to succeed," said Andrew. "Look at the way they sell lumber in town. No place to store it, no lumber yard like we had in Mobile. They get it from the boat and just haul it around. Several frame buildings are going up already."

Regina and the children went looking in the other stores, while Andrew went to the barber shop. The owner was Peter Biggs. Peter was a Negro and had once been a slave. He was sold to an officer at Fort Leavenworth and was freed at the close of the Mexican War. He came to California and opened his shop on Main Street near the Bella Union Hotel. Since there was only one high-backed chair, the men sat waiting their turn. As Biggs called, "Next," he sprinkled his last customer with Florida water and at the same time applied his homemade concoction of bear oil as a finishing touch. Watching the man being doused with bear oil, another waiting customer led Andrew aside and said, "Don't let Peter put that bear oil on you. It stains the pillows. My wife gives me fits if I go home with it on." Andrew thanked him, sat down, and dozed off. When Andrew's turn came, the man sitting next to him gave him a nudge and up he sprang. He got into the chair, Peter cut his hair, gave him a treatment of Florida water and before Andrew had a chance to object, Peter gave him a sprinkling of bear oil.

Back at the Plaza, Andrew rejoined Regina and the children as they were coming out of Harris Newmark's store. Andrew had promised to take his family to the Bella Union Hotel for the noonday meal. It was the town's leading hotel, saloon, and restaurant, as well as the favorite meeting place. Henry Hammel had recently added a second story and it was now advertised far and wide as "one of California's finest."

Just then, they heard the shrill steam whistle on the rooftop, letting both transients and regulars alike know their meal was ready. They walked over and waited in line outside the door. People came scurrying from all directions, crowding around to be the first to enter.

After lunch, as they returned to the street, the children watched an ice wagon as it came lumbering into town, dripping water out the back. Being winter, huge blocks of ice were cut in the distant mountains and hauled to town. During the summer, the ice had to be brought down from Alaska in chunks, packed in straw. Don Abel Stearns was one of the few who could afford it.

Regina suddenly felt faint; Andrew steadied her. A man walking nearby hurried over, dipped his handkerchief in the water trough and put it on her forehead. As soon as Regina felt better, Andrew took her home.

It was the day after Christmas. Their third child was due momentarily. Regina and Andrew had agreed on the name of Regina if the baby was a girl. The name had been in the family for five generations; however, they were going to call her "Jenny" to save confusion. If it was a boy, they were going to call him George. Dr. Griffin, who was always very busy, was on hand to help with the delivery.

"Oh, doctor, I'm so glad you're here," said Regina.

"I wanted to be here, Regina. I have to take special care of you. Andrew, If you would step outside for a bit, Regina and I have a job to do."

"I'm on my way Doctor, but say the word and I'll come on the run," figuring he'd better hurry.

After the baby arrived, the doctor said, "You'll be in good hands now Regina, with Mrs. Childs and Jesse to look after you." He went outside to give Andrew the good news. Andrew was out in the shed pacing up and down. Anxious to hear about the baby, he rushed over to the doctor coming through the door.

"It's a girl, Andrew. Regina is fine. I understand you're calling her Jenny. She's a beauty, all right."

"How soon can I see them?"

"It'll be a little while. The womenfolk are finishing up a bit."

Regina Weinshank

CHAPTER IX

A few month later, an epidemic of smallpox broke out in Los Angeles and spread like wildfire throughout the town. It took a large toll of lives. Deaths were so frequent, the city fathers asked the padres to stop ringing the church bells for the souls of the departed. Baptisms were postponed because the priests were busy burying the dead. Yellow flags marked the adobes where the dreaded disease struck, letting others know that the families were in quarantine. The smallpox wagon, the "Black Maria," was a frequent sight as it moved slowly down Fort Street past the Weinshank adobe. Funeral processions were long and fatiguing, the men on horseback, the women on foot. Few Indians survived the white man's disease. As many as fifteen to twenty a day died on the ranchos and in town.

Regina worked from morning to night, going from house to house, supervising the care of the sick. Her other work would have to wait. She assisted at births, taking it upon herself to baptize the babies. She feared they too would contract the dread disease and die before they could be baptized by the overworked padres. Her selfless work caring for others earned her the title, "The Angel of Los Angeles."

The Sisters of Charity established a hospital in the quiet, airy part of town north of the church in a small adobe belonging to Cristobal Aquilar. Some of the stricken townfolk were taken there, but most were cared for at home. Dr. Walter Lindley almost single-handedly vaccinated those who had not been stricken with the dread disease. The serum came from Joseph Downey's drugstore, the only one between San Francisco and San Diego.

"What is this, Doctor?" asked Regina as she watched Dr. Lindley inoculate a patient she was caring for.

"It's called a vaccination. It's a serum taken from those who have already had the disease. The vaccination causes the body to become immune to smallpox."

"Would you be able to come by our house and vaccinate my family?"

"The sooner the better. If you're leaving now, I'll be right over."

"I'm leaving in just a minute, Doctor."

As soon as Regina walked in the door at home, she said, "Gather around children. The doctor is coming to scratch your arm and put a drop of serum on it."

The doctor followed her in.

"I'm going to put it in their hips, Regina. It can leave an ugly scar."

Carrie looked to her mother for reassurance. Regina walked over to her and held her hands while the doctor lifted her skirt and administered the shot. Little Frank sent up a howl. The neighbors the country over could hear him. Andrew stepped up and then it was Regina's turn.

Days following the vaccination, the family felt slightly ill and moped around the house. A crust formed over the scratches and left big, ugly scars. When Regina had a chance, she talked to the doctor. "We all felt so bum after that vaccination, doctor."

"That proves it was a good thing to get those vaccinations, Regina. It shows that if you had gotten smallpox, you could have died from it. You're very lucky."

Tom Rowan stopped by to deliver bread from his father's bakery. As he walked through the door, the doctor called to him. "Tom, get over here and let me give you a vaccination."

"I don't need that sir. I'm not sick," answered Tom.

"Get over here anyway, that's when it's most effective. This way we'll all feel better about it. Anyway, working in the bakery you are more apt to spread germs."

"All right. I'll do it, but first promise it won't hurt!"

"Well, not too much at any rate."

The great floods of the previous winter were followed by several dry seasons, bringing on a drought, giving Los Angeles the appearance of a desert wasteland. The lean, long-horn cattle staggered across the barren hills and died from lack of water.

Thousands of cattle perished, leaving the hillsides littered with their sun bleached bones. With their cattle and crops wiped out, many of the rancheros lost their land. Don Abel Stearns was forced to mortgage his Rancho Los Alamitos. Don Julio Verdugo let his taxes accumulate, until he lost his rancho. Ricardo Vejar lost his property by foreclosure. In town, the merchants became downhearted. The collector of taxes was unable to collect a single cent. The floods and drought had taken their toll.

With the squatters, the money lenders, and the farmers moving in, the days of the ranchos were numbered. The romantic era of the ranchos had lasted throughout the 1830s, the 40s and the 50s. Now in the 60s, they were doomed.

About the author

REGINA PHELAN graduated from Whittier College in 1942. Fifth in her family to major in physical education, she completed her credential work in that field five years later after teaching at Hudson School in La Puente.

She spent many years teaching physical education at the high school level in the Norwalk-La Mirada School District.

It might be said that she followed in the footsteps of her grandfather, Henry Charles Lee, the English circus man, in choosing her profession, for according to the well known circus historian, George Chindahl, physical education is the outgrowth of the circus.

It was for the love of her family and of her state that Regina Phelan wrote this book.

About the illustrator

Al Champy, based in New Jersey, has studied fine arts as well as commercial arts and is a professional photographer. He has worked for advertising agencies and for several years operated his own but the creative fulfillment sought was not to be his until he decided to downsize to a more personalized art studio. Twenty five years have passed but Brookwood Studio continues to be a fountain of creativity to a man, who as a boy, dreamed of becoming an artist.